T(w)o Bits

Loves, losses, and lenses

Melissa Zoller

Val,

I hope you enjoy!

To Sandi and Nisha:

You caused this.

To K, M, T, C, J, B, M, J, and P:

You're not blameless, either.

At some point, the sun will break through

Even the darkest clouds don't hover forever

So be kind to yourself

Keep your eyes open

Even the longest night breaks at the end

When the sun starts to set at the north pole

(usually around my birthday, so take that for what it is)

It also starts to rise in the south

And, a few weeks after mom's birthday, the perspective reverses

And the dark becomes day again

All this just to say:

I've seen you washed in the sun's rays

And you're perfect.

At some point, the stars will shine again
Even the hottest summer doesn't swelter ad infinitum
So be kind to yourself
Hydrate and eat well
Even the longest day is only twenty-four hours
When the sun starts to rise at the south pole
(usually around my birthday, so take that for what it is)
It also starts to set in the north
And, a few weeks after mom's birthday, the perspective reverses
And the day becomes light again

All this just to say:
I've seen you dance in the moonlight
And you're perfect.

If you think this is about you, it probably is
But the scars that I live in, they're not yours, they're his

But it was your breath on my neck
And it was your voice in my ear
Your hand on my waist
And your footsteps walking away

I've been lucky
I think
Up to now, I've never understood
When people have said
How *cold* it can be
How *dark*
How *empty*
And how *quickly* it comes about
When someone turns away

I've been lucky
I think
Up to now, I've never known
That particular heartache
How *lost* you can feel
How *unseen*
How *forgotten*
And how *unexpectedly* it hit my heart
When someone turned away

I've been lucky
I think
I'm not so lucky
Anymore

Look for me in open windows

Look for me in solemn nights

Look for me in silent prayer

Look for me in glimmering lights

I'll be there

I'll be there in the comfort and I'll be there in the pain

I'll be there, beaming love, when we meet again

Until then, look for me and I'll be there

before you praise her strength
remember what it cost her
because being strong
is almost always forced on us against our will
and a non-exhaustive list
of everything she's survived
might look a lot like mine
might look a lot like yours
might include assault
might include heartbreak
might include loss
might include the broken

and if you're only here
to be just another someone she survived
then
move along

admire her strength

but don't praise her for it
she never wanted it in the first place

(16)

she deserves to be soft
sometimes

Anyways

I ♥ y

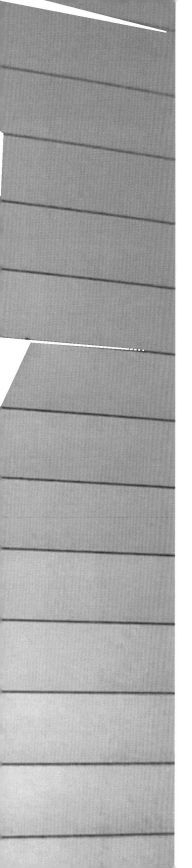

Maybe I'm too late
(*I probably am*)
But I still buy greeting cards for your
birthday
My first instinct is still to text you in
the morning
(*And the evening, and the afternoon*)
But I know I get up earlier than you
So I never do, and the moment passes

Maybe I'm too late
(*I probably am*)
But I still look for your name
My first thought is still you in the
morning
(*and the evening, and the afternoon*)
But I know I started earlier than you
So I never call, and the moment passes

Maybe I'm too late
(*I probably am*)
But if I'm not

I made this for you. Can you believe what he said? I think I need a new job. I applied for that job. I didn't get that job. I miss you. Remember the coyotes? I'm just tired today, that's all. There've been a lot of broken promises. Did I send you this meme before? F*ck, I love red pandas. Let's move to Scotland. Do you think they'll ever figure it out? I don't know why he didn't choose you. He's an idiot. It's her loss. Do you want to go for a hike? I need some help with this P&L. We all need a break. Every single one of them cancelled. I just feel like stomping is the right thing to do in this situation. I'm high, so high, right now. I miss your face. We should build a treehouse. I adore those shoes. No, I don't like sushi, but I'm sure they serve something else, too. I brought coffee.

And other love stories between friends.

If step one is to meet
And step two is to lust
Then steps three, four, and five
Probably work towards trust

But if step six is to love
And step seven's back to lust
Then I lost you at eight
Between pedestal and dust

And here we are at nine
And it seems an abyss
So can we skip ten through twelve
And restart at a kiss?

Because thirteen seems lucky
And the next dozen, too
So maybe, here's hoping,
Twenty-five slams me back into you.

Forever sounded
like home when
you said it.

They say we don't grow from what's easy
That a challenge is what we need

But that's the paradox with us
Loving you has always been the simplest thing in the world
Yet I've never grown more than in your arms

A near miss in aviation is still a five-hundred-foot distance
When you're looking at asteroids, it's over 1.5 million miles

So what would you call
What happened to us?
When you could fit one, maybe two,
But definitely not three breaths between us

And still, we went our separate ways

And I miss you every day

I've loved you in every lifetime

But for today
I'll speed down the highway
With Lewis Capaldi on repeat
And I'll pretend that I'm okay

With being someone you loved

In a former life

I dream of surprise continuances after acres of endings

You'll arrive without notice And wait on the porch (*I'll have a porch*) (*I'll be out buying groceries when you get there*) And I'll see you as I pull up

And you'll grin, and I'll smile And you'll kiss my cheek and I'll wrap around your neck And I'll take the groceries while you grab your luggage And we'll have coffee inside (*Or maybe tea on the deck*) And we'll talk for ages And fall asleep on the couch

And I'll brush my teeth While you're in the shower And maybe we'll go for a walk And laugh about who we were And I'll trace the lines in your hands And you'll clear the mugs And I'll pray you don't notice (*Or maybe that you do*) That the laughlines are deeper now And that's mostly because of you

And I'll go slowly down the stairs Just to have an extra minute And I'll pause on the second-last step Just to soak in your profile

And it'll be simple like calculus And it'll be hard like a breeze But it will be us It will be us It'll be us (*in a dream*)

(33)

I am no longer interested in unspoken
And no longer pretending to be unbroken
Just to be found and lost again

I am no longer interested in whispered
And no longer pretending I've been misheard
Just to be found and lost again

Anything less than loud
Isn't welcome here
Anymore

If epiphany is spiritual realization,
then God is in the seeker, not the sought
and God is in the curious, not the known
and God is in the fighter, not the fought,
and God is in the music, not the dance,
and you are holy, you are holy, you are holy,
and I am not

And if epiphany is spiritual realization
then God is in the newness, not the same,
and God is in the seer, not the seen,
and God is in the breaking, not the tame,
and you are holy, you are holy, you are holy,
when you speak my name

Hold on to the little griefs
The dropped-the-call-before-saying-I-love-you's
The grocery-store-was-out-of-it-sorry's
The someone-I-chose-chose-someone-else's
The I-didn't-get-the-job's
The bought-it-before-it-was-on-sale's
The my-favourite-shirt-has-a-hole-in-it's

The little griefs

Not the world-ending devastation
Not the heart-breaking cataclysm
The little world-alterers
The little heart-changers

The little ones

Hold on to them
Live in them
Breathe them

Then let them go

The three saddest words in the English language:

I used to.

I used to love him.

I used to know her.

I used to be fun.

I used to smile.

I used to know what to do.

I used to know how to be.

I used to know where to go.

I used to know who to trust.

I used to be okay.

Can I put you in a locket?
Can I place you at the hollow of my throat
        Where your lips should be?

You can rest there
        With all the words we haven't said
                With all the breath we haven't shared

Can I put you in a locket?
Can I wrap you around my neck
        Where your arms should be?

Can I put you in a locket?
        Slightly tarnished over time
Can I put you in my locket?
Can I maybe call you mine?

Thank you for making me love

        all the parts of me

                you couldn't.

Thank you for being there, and for trying to make it right

Thank you for seeing me, but leaving without a fight

Thank you for stopping by, and not staying too long

Thank you for introducing me to my new favourite song

Thank you for showing me everything I've missed

Thank you for coming back, I'm so grateful you exist

I love books with broken spines
Dog-eared pages
Soft edges
Crinkled covers
Well-thumbed chapters
Highlighted sections
Notes in margins

Because they hold stories
Beyond the author's
Stories of love and laughter
Of tears and tragedies
Of sitting in a train station
And under the covers with a flashlight
Stories of rain on windows
And snow on eyelashes
Of tea and tablet
And hot chocolate with mallows

I will.

I am.

I can.

And I do.

I am a chaos gardener

I sow my mint directly in the ground

I let my raspberries grow too tall

I never have a plan

I throw seeds wherever the wind takes them

I'm delighted when something takes root

The problem is,

I do the same with people I love

I let seeds settle where they wish

And I'm still delighted when something takes root

And I'm still surprised when something flourishes

And I still love the seeds that never surface

Everyone she's ever loved has left.

"That's just how life goes - everyone has to say goodbye."

No.

Not like this.
Out the window in the bathroom while she's dressing.
Out the passenger side while she's shifting gears.
Out the back door while she's walking in the front.

Everyone she's ever loved has left.
And none of them ever said goodbye.

Repurpose her
From stranger to friend to lover to life
From lover to partner to forgotten ex-wife
From partner to lost to stranger again
Recycle her heart, hallelujah, amen

Because if that's all she is: just a thing to be used
An object to be craved, fondled, hurt, and abused
If her stories of terror have kept you amused
And her mute screams of anguish have left you unbruised

Then repurpose her
From stranger to captive to pressed underboot
From captive to freed to forbidden ripe fruit
From freed to forgotten to stranger again
Recycle her life, hallelujah, amen

Leave the story discarded
From the villain's perspective

I still think I'll turn around and see you in the crowd.

Eight billion people, and yours is the only face I seek.

What does it say about me that I just want to look at you?

That I started drowning the second we met?

That, not even for a second, did I ever think to reach for the raft?

What does it say about me that you still make me weak?

And someday I'll have baskets of fruit to share with
anyone who asks

And my table will be long enough to feed anyone who
shows up

And if it's not long enough, I'll sit on the floor and eat
from a paper plate so you can be full

And there will be laughter and joy and hands in the dirt

And you can stay as long as you want, come and go as
you need

But you'll never leave hungry

I still don't know how to look at you
And not see the August sun rising
But the moon is out and
The stars are shining and
Aurora dancing and
Comets shooting and
Snow falling

So find me where the sun sets
And let me melt into you
If only for a moment
In the red and burnt blue of dusk
Before midnight

Wilden your horizons
Go feral
Chase goosebumps
Run with wolves
Make magic and make love
Smile more, say less, use your hands
Taste freedom and savour it
Stretch your fingers
Mark your own true north
Never give in (*unless giving in means an open heart*)
Never surrender (*unless surrender means a messy bed*)
Say *I love you* more
Forget the makeup
Let the wind take your hair
Embrace your chaos
Race the sunset home
One hand on the wheel
One hand in mine
Wilden your horizons

Hindsight is 20/20
So believe me now when I say
You were always more of a dream than a real person
(*And I don't mean that in a nice way*)
The kind of dream that leaves sheets soaked
Hair a mess, legs quaking
But a dream that dissipated
IMMEDIATELY
Upon waking

The way you reached out to me
Hands and words so achingly tender
Had me believing there was more to you
Than just that nighttime splendor
Fool me once, shame on you,
But fool me twice and the shame is mine
If you ever discover depth in love
Maybe that will be our time
If you never do, then you do you
I love you, *truly*, but I don't need this from you

This one's for the lover girls and boss bitches
For the passenger princesses and moss witches
For the ones who grew strong as a way to survive
For the ones for whom softness makes them feel more alive
For the too much, too loud, taking too much space
For the quiet, the small, the always in their place
For the moms and the aunts and the daughters and sisters
For the missus and the misses and the Mx and the Mr's
For the readers of smut and STEM journal authors
(from toddling in diapers to racing with walkers)
For the lehdies, the feminine, affirmed or assigned
For the hot mess, the calm, the destroyed, the aligned
For the ones wielding tools made for calloused hands
For the lipsticked, the bombshells, the hopeful "Yes, and"s
For the graceless, the messy, the "I'm just a token"
For the back-pocket girlfriends, the unbowed, unbroken
For the rusty, the dusty, the always put together
For the built like a brick shithouse, for the light as a feather
For the ones who are doubtful, lonely, adored
For the ones who will accept being anything but bored
For the ones doing it all and the ones protecting peace
For the ones who are owning their own damn release
For the ones wearing pink, red, orange, black, or blue
For the ones standing naked, this one's for you

May you lift up, assist, sometimes follow, sometimes lead
May you process and grow at your own goddamned speed
(And to those who'd complain, may you pay them no heed)

May you *know*, *love*, and *be* the woman you need

I need you... Well I could just leave it at that.
It's no less true for being only half a thought.
But the whole thing is
(*the whole messy, unfair, absurd, gut-wrenching thing*)

I need you to say my name.
Whisper it, scream it, ~~type it out~~ don't type it out because that
doesn't work. I need to hear my name in your voice.

I need you to want to, to try to, to actually be here.
With me. Just the two of us, however that looks.

I need you to need me,
but I'm so used to being needed that I need you to want me, too.
Equal measures, one more than the other (at times), just let me feel
that for once.

I need you to grab me,
to shake me, to do whatever it takes for you to be confident that you
have my undivided attention, and then I need you to say in plain
English that you choose me, or you want to explore this thing, or
that you think about me almost as much as I think about you.

I need you is the half a thought.

But the whole thing is

I could love you so easily - *so easily* - which is nonsensical and beyond reason but no less true for being only my side of the story.

I called joy back to me
And she showed up with friends
Here she hosted favours
There a quiet form of amends

For the days I lay wasted
And unable to move
Joy brought me to myself
Joy had nothing to prove

I called hope back to me
And she arrived with a yell
Something soft, something whispered,
Something about being through hell

For the days I sat silent
And unable to speak
Hope brought me to myself
Hope was everything but weak

I called love back to me
And she rolled in on a smile
She glinted and grinned
"Hey, girl, it's been awhile"

For the days I stood stoic
And unable to break through
Love brought me to myself
Love brought me you

He left a bruise on my soul
But you left a torn-off dress, welded to the floor
He stole a bit of my time
But you, you became everything and nothing more

He left his hat in my bed
But you left a blanket fort, dismantled on the chair
He stole a bit of my smile
But you, you replaced all breathable air

He had a glint in his eye, but you brought back laughter
He was the flood, but you,
      You were the umbrella in the rafters

The wind isn't howling tonight
It's screeching
After too long baking
Under searing skies
It's frenetic and desperate
A necessary release of energy
Leaves and hair whipped and pulled

The wind isn't sighing tonight
It's begging
After too long silent
Not given voice
It's ember-burnt and aflame
A necessary change of pace
Flags and jackets pulled and torn

Love, why are you outside in this?
Love, why are you fighting the wind?
You should come inside
I wish you were inside

You looked an awful lot like forever

And you felt an awful lot like home

But somewhere under fireworks

I still walked the night alone

Any space I cleared for you in this fragmented heart
Will always be yours
You are the art

If you leave and then come back, no matter how long
It's still yours to live in
The bones are still strong

Clear cobwebs, repaint - this is your home
The love's always there
You're never alone

I'm always leaving doors open and lights on
(but I can build walls just fine)

They're just friends.

(She still says his name like a prayer)
(He still smells her perfume when he smiles)
(She still sees his face in a sigh)
(He still holds his breath like her hand)

Just friends.

I took off the red string that tethered me to you

I didn't need scissors, it wanted to leave

Knots came undone on their own

I guess it was time to be unmoored

And you know something?

No anchor feels a lot like drifting

Away from shore, no land in sight

At the mercy of currents I don't understand

Under skies I don't have memorized

But under fear of the unknown is something sweet

It tastes almost like cinnamon sugar

It's not loneliness, not quite

And not freedom, not quite

But maybe somewhere between

But maybe peace and place and future

But maybe, just me

Play me like a piano
Strum me like a guitar
Verse, chorus, bridge,
And then we'll figure out where we are

Because I write you like a symphony
But you sing me like a dirge

So play me like a cello
Rosined bow across the strings
Bridge, chorus, verse
And we'll get lost in musical things

Because I write you like a symphony
But you sing me like a dirge

So play me like a love song
That gentle roll across the snare
Verse, bridge, chorus
Find the coda, find me there

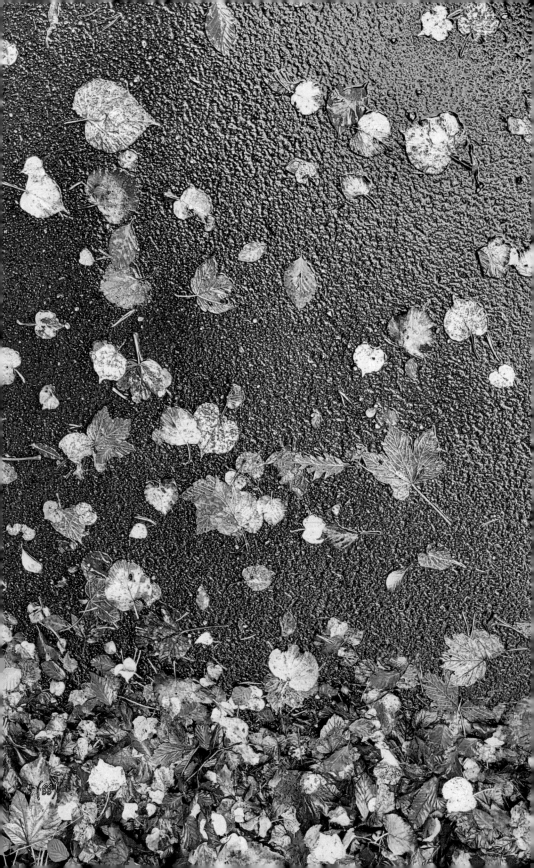

And so, if the last time we spoke is to be the last time we ever speak,

And if the last time we held each other is to be the last time we ever touch,

And if the last time we danced is to be the last time the song plays,

And if the last time we laughed together is to be the last smile we share,

I hope you carry with you,

Until the moon falls and the sun fades,

One simple truth:

You were loved by me.